Virginia B.

GOES TO THE SYMPHONY

Virginia B. Goes to the Symphony
By: Kevin Pease

Published by:
VJ PUBLISHING HOUSE, LLC.
20451 NW 2nd Avenue Suite 112
Miami Gardens, Florida 33169
Phone: 786-303-9551

www.vjpublishinghouse.com
vjpublishinghouse@gmail.com

Illustrations by: Gabriel Gigliotti

© 2025, June

Paperback ISBN: 978-1-939236-23-4
Hardcover ISBN: 978-1-939236-22-7
eBook ISBN: 978-1-939236-24-1
Series One

Virginia B.

GOES TO THE SYMPHONY

By Kevin Pease

Illustrations by Gabriel Gigliotti

This book is dedicated to **Virginia B. Toulmin** who built a profound legacy not with grand pronouncements, but through a life shaped by quiet grace, unwavering generosity, and deep faith.

Virginia's commitment to leading by example lives on through her foundation, which faithfully upholds her vision by championing organizations that make a meaningful difference in communities both near and far.

The stories in the Virginia B. series imagine the early origins of the qualities that made adult Virginia such a remarkable spirit. We hope her adventures inspire young readers to use their time, talents, and voices to help create a kinder, more generous, and more beautiful world. What better legacy could one ask for?

Welcome to the world of Virginia B. I'm so glad you're here.

Bill Villafranco

Trustee, Virginia B. Toulmin Foundation

CHAPTER 1

It was a surprisingly pleasant late-February day in St. Louis, Missouri. A winter chill lingered in the air, but the sun hung low, casting long, golden shadows over the stately brick manors lining the street. Bob walked his younger sister home from school, his stride steady and purposeful. As usual, ten-year-old Virginia trailed a few steps behind, her nose buried in a book.

"Come on, Gin. We can't be late... again."

She sighed, adjusting her pace, just enough to show she was listening, but not enough to fully satisfy her brother. Her eyes stayed fixed on the page in front of her.

As they turned left onto Gustine Street, Bob

nudged her again. "You know, Gin, Großmutter (grandmother) will be expecting us. She gets cross when we're late."

That did the trick. Virginia snapped her book closed with a dramatic flourish and, with a few long strides, fell in step beside her brother.

"What are you reading anyway? It must be something special to keep you so distracted."

Virginia didn't answer immediately. Instead, she took his hand and closed her eyes for a moment. The distant clang of the 4th Street cable car rang in her ears, mixing with the rustling leaves and the laughter of children playing near Tower Grove Park. Together, these sounds were a melody, a song only she could hear.

Begrudgingly, she opened her eyes. "I was studying mathematics, *Robert.*" She was the only one who ever called her brother by his full name. "And don't call me Gin. You know I prefer Virginia." She let go of his hand, pulled out her book, and immersed herself in it again just as they turned onto Hartford

Street.

Clang clang… clang clang. The bell on the cable car rang out, its sharp notes lingering in the crisp air.

"See Robert? We're home!"

He chuckled, shaking his head. "You and your numbers, Gin. I just don't get it."

Virginia flashed a wide smile at her big brother, shrugged, and bounded up the twelve steps to their front door, leaving Robert on the sidewalk below.

As the front door swung open, she inhaled deeply. She could smell the primroses that Mother kept in a ceramic vase just inside the foyer and the scent of the freshly polished mahogany staircase. And then there it was—the smell she had been hoping for: cinnamon. They weren't too late after all.

"Hallo! Oma! We're home!"

CHAPTER 2

"Ich bin in der Küche. Begleite mich, meine Zuckermund!" ("I'm in the kitchen; join me, my little sugar mouth!")

Meine Zuckermund; My little sugar mouth. It had been Oma's pet name for Virginia from the time she was a little girl. Virginia had an insatiable sweet tooth, like her Großmutter, her Oma.

"Coming, Oma!" Virginia hurried into the kitchen, where her Oma stood with her hands on her hips and a crisp, flowered apron around her waist. Oma Tilly had come to live with Virginia's family after her Großvater (grandfather) Opa Emil had passed away two years earlier. Virginia loved coming home to find her Oma waiting.

Oma looked her granddaughter up and down as she entered the kitchen, her hands still on her hips and a stern look on her face.

"Mein Gott im Himmel! Wie kann das sein? ("My God in Heaven! How can this be?") You've grown six inches taller since breakfast!"

Virginia giggled. "Oma! I'm the same height as always. You're teasing me!"

"Wenn du darauf bestehst," ("If you insist,") Oma sighed dramatically. "It must be these old eyes playing tricks on me. Now, meine Zuckermund, you can help me with the baking while you tell me all about your day."

Dutifully, Virginia dropped her books on the kitchen table, put on her favorite apron—pale yellow with white stripes—and climbed onto her stool. Oma handed her a smooth wooden spoon.

"Stir," Oma directed. Virginia plunged the spoon deep into the ceramic bowl before her. A cloud of flour and spices rose up, filling the air with rich scents of cinnamon, nutmeg, and sugar.

"Oma!" Virginia inhaled deeply. "Is this your Zimt-Kaffeekuchen? Your cinnamon coffee cake?" Oma made the best Kuchen, a sweet German cake. In the summer, she topped the cake with sour cherries; in the fall, she used tart apples. But Oma's cinnamon coffee cake was the best of all.

"Ja, meine Zuckermund. Zimt-Kaffeekuchen— your favorite. Now... tell me about your day."

Virginia beamed. "Today was my mathematics examination."

"And?" Oma prompted.

"And —" Virginia continued, not missing a beat, "I received top marks in the class! Not a single answer was incorrect! My teacher says that I have a remarkable mind for numbers."

Oma clapped her hands. "That you do! Du machst mich stolz." ("You make me proud.") She ruffled Virginia's hair. "Now, enough stirring. Use that remarkable mind of yours and measure the butter."

Virginia slid off the stool and fetched the heavy

butter crock from the larder. She carried the crock to the kitchen table and lifted the bell-shaped lid to reveal a block of pale-yellow butter. "How much do we need, Oma?" Virginia asked over her shoulder.

"Alright, alright. Lassen sie mich sehen." ("let me see.") Oma paced around the kitchen in small circles as she searched her memory for the answer. (Oma didn't write down any of her recipes.) As she moved in a figure-eight pattern across the kitchen floor, flour and sugar fell from her apron onto the ground like tiny snowflakes. She stopped suddenly, throwing her hands in the air. "Ah! Ich erinnere mich!" ("I remember!") "170 grams for the batter and another 60 grams for the topping."

Virginia smirked. "Oma, in the United States, we use ounces, not grams."

Oma bent down, bringing her nose close to her granddaughter's. "I know that meine Zuckermund. Du bist schlau. ("But you're clever.") Figure it out!" She winked.

Virginia winked back. "Let's see. If one ounce

equals... approximately 28 grams, we would need..." She did some quick calculations, only partially using her fingers. "Six ounces of butter for the batter and another two ounces for my favorite part—the crumbly topping."

Oma raised an eyebrow, challenging her granddaughter. "Bist du sicher?" ("Are you certain?")

Virginia puffed out her chest. "Yes. Ich bin mir sicher." ("I am certain.")

Oma smiled, filled with pride, and carefully measured the butter, cutting it into tiny bits before returning the crock to its place in the larder. As they worked in silence, Virginia relished this moment. This was her special time with Oma—just the two of them.

"Braves Mädchen." ("Good girl.") Oma patted Virginia on the head as she began incorporating the butter into the dry ingredients in her bowl. They worked silently for a few moments, Virginia stirring and Oma measuring. Virginia was grateful for this time with Oma. Robert wasn't as fond of speaking German as Virginia was, and a small part of her was thankful for that. It meant she had Oma all to herself.

As they worked a thought occurred to Virginia. "Oma? You usually only make Kuchen for special occasions. What's the occasion?"

Oma chuckled, pulling Virginia into a warm hug. "So *klug*." ("So *smart*.") Have patience. Your Oma's secrets will reveal themselves in time. Now, off to practice your piano. Supper will be ready soon."

Virginia sighed but obeyed. She removed her apron, placing it atop her stool and gave her Oma a big hug. As she left the kitchen, the scent of cinnamon lingered, wrapping her in warmth. Whatever Oma's secret was, she couldn't *wait* to find out.

CHAPTER 3

Virginia made her way from the kitchen through the front entrance hall and turned right into the family drawing room, which was located at the front of the house. The drawing room was warm and sunny, with comfortable seating arranged around a brick fireplace crowned with a polished wooden mantle. This was the room where the Bernthal family welcomed guests and gathered after supper to talk and play cards.

Opposite the fireplace, along a short wall was Mama's piano, one of Virginia's most favorite things in the Bernthal home. Her Papa, William Bernthal, had purchased the Kieselhorst upright piano as a wedding gift for his bride in 1919. Virginia's Mama, Edna Bernthal, had loved music her entire life, a passion she shared with her daughter. She and her husband had been born in the late 19th century, a time of significant economic and cultural growth for St. Louis. The city thrived on steamboat commerce, and another wave of prosperity took hold as railroads emerged. A hallmark of an upwardly mobile middle-class family in St. Louis was the presence of a piano in the home. Between 1890 and 1900, the number of pianos in private residences grew at a rate five times faster than before. By the turn of the century, more than a million American households owned pianos. Virginia was proud that there was such a magnificent instrument in their home.

Mama adored the Kieselhorst piano and took great care in polishing its handsome ebony case, which featured ornate carvings of vines and flowers. Virginia grew up surrounded by music. She loved sitting on her mother's lap as Mama played popular parlor songs of the day such as "Home Sweet Home," "O Promise Me," and Virginia's favorite, "K-K-K-Katy," which always made her giggle when Papa sang it in his rich baritone. When she was a little girl, Virginia would rest her hands atop her mother's as Mama played, pretending she was making the music. It was no surprise when Virginia declared she was ready to begin lessons shortly after her sixth birthday.

Virginia proved to be a quick study on the piano. She loved running her fingers along the smooth ivory and black wooden keys, gliding from the top of the keyboard to the bottom. At first, she found it frustrating that her feet barely reached the pedals, but Mama assured her that she would grow into them soon enough. Virginia cherished the keys where the ivory had been worn down slightly—evidence of her mother's graceful touch over the years.

As for her own playing, Virginia prided herself on her accuracy at the keyboard. She adapted easily to lessons, with her mother as her first piano teacher. She started with scales, first with her right hand and then her left, moving slowly up and down the keys until she could play both hands together. Once she had mastered the major key signatures, she moved on to the more intricate minor keys and eventually the chromatic scales. Mama had also promised to teach her the jazz scales—the seductive patterns of notes that formed the foundation of America's newest musical obsession: swing.

In no time at all, Virginia mastered hymns, Christmas carols, and even Mozart's "Minuet and Rondo," but her very favorite pieces were always Bach's Inventions—especially those he had written for his wife, Anna Magdalena. Virginia's mathematical mind delighted in how the melodies intertwined, with musical ideas spiraling into one another, each phrase transforming and leading into something new.

Memorization came easily to Virginia. Once she had committed a piece to memory, she would often close her eyes while playing, allowing Bach's melodies to build in her imagination, layer upon layer— constructing towers of sound that stretched to the sky. She was lost in one of these musical daydreams when her brother's voice pulled her back to reality.

"Gin, it's suppertime."

Virginia sighed, slowly opened her eyes, and then stood. Carefully, she pushed herself off the heavy wooden bench, closed her beloved music notebook for Anna Magdalena Bach, and ran her fingers over the title.

Someday, she thought, *someday I will be a great musician like Anna Magdalena and play in a grand concert hall.*

With that, she gently lowered the lid over the keyboard, smoothed out her skirt and headed to supper.

CHAPTER 4

Virginia was passing through the foyer on her way from the parlor to the dining room when, like clockwork, the front door swung open.

"Good evening, Papa!" Virginia beamed as her father stepped through the door. She ran to him and wrapped her arms around his waist for a quick hug before stepping back to take him in. Her Papa, was a handsome man with kind eyes, always dressed sharply in a vest and bow tie.

Papa arrived home promptly each evening at 5:15 PM, and Virginia loved being the first to greet him. She also adored visiting him at work downtown. His office, nestled in a grand corner of the St. Louis-San Francisco Railroad corporate building, boasted tall windows overlooking bustling Olive Street. There, she would sit at his massive desk, clacking away on his adding machine, and pretending to be a businesswoman. Papa always said she had inherited her knack for numbers from him.

"How was your day, Virginia?" he asked warmly as they made their way into the dining room together. Oma and Robert were already seated at the table.

"You'll be proud of me, Papa. I received the highest marks in class on our mathematics examination — a 99%."

From across the dining table, Oma winked at her. Virginia winked back.

"A 99%! That's marvelous, Virginia. With just a little extra effort, I'm certain you could earn a perfect 100% next time." He tousled her blonde curls.

Virginia sighed, placing her hands on her hips. Papa immediately recognized the stance and braced himself for one of his youngest child's famous lectures.

"Actually, Papa, I did earn a 100%. In fact, I've scored 100% on every mathematics examination this year."

Papa crossed *his* arms and tilted his head, mirroring her pose. A small smirk spread across his lips, which he tried to suppress; she was so earnest and full of spirit.

"I'm confused Virginia. If you have scored 100% on all of your exams why did you tell me you earned a 99%?" he asked.

Virginia's eyes twinkled.

"My teacher asked to speak with me before I left the classroom today," she explained. "She told me that while I earned a perfect score on every test, when she writes my final grade, it won't say 100."

Papa frowned, bemused. "Why not?"

She shrugged. "It's simply *not* done, Papa. So, my report card will say 99."

Papa threw his hands in the air. "That makes no sense at all."

Virginia smiled, crinkling her nose. "I thought the same thing, but you know what, Papa. I know the truth, which is good enough for me."

Virginia turned and retreated to her chair next to Robert and directly across the table from Oma.

William shook his head, laughing softly. He was in awe of her confidence. *Spirit*, he thought. *That girl is going to change the world.*

Friday evenings at the Bernthal home were always special, and tonight was no exception. Mama took great pride in maintaining a proper home. The dining table was a solid mahogany Duncan Phyfe that gleamed under the glow of the chandelier. When their house was built, Papa had carefully selected most of their sturdy, mission-style furniture from the Lammert Furniture Company, just a few blocks north of his office in downtown St. Louis.

But the dining room table was exceptional—a cherished wedding gift from Mama's grandparents, who had traveled from New York City to settle in Missouri. Its rectangular tabletop with softly rounded corners, exuded elegance, and years of Mama's diligent polishing had deepened the wood into a rich red hue. The table was supported by two graceful pedestal bases, each with three curved legs ending in solid brass casters. Virginia loved dinnertime with her family, and sitting at this table made her feel special... almost fancy.

The table was set tonight with the family's finest china and crystal stemware. Virginia's eyes widened as she took in the spread—red cabbage, potato dumplings, and, to her surprise, her favorite: Mama's famous sauerbraten. Her stomach rumbled.

Sauerbraten? she thought. *On a regular Friday night? That was a meal reserved for special occasions. Something must be going on.*

Edna Bernthal, a lithe, graceful woman, entered the room carrying a tray of roast. She floated to her seat at the far end of the table, pausing only to kiss the tops of her children's heads. With quiet elegance, she pulled out her chair, sat down, and placed her linen napkin on her lap.

Her sharp eyes scanned the room. "Who will lead us in saying grace?"

"I led last night," Robert groaned. "It's Gin's turn."

Virginia opened her mouth to protest, but Papa shot her a look—*the* look. It stopped any rebuttal.

"I do believe Robert is right. Virginia, it's your turn."

Virginia straightened in her chair. "Yes, Papa." She clasped hands with her family, bowed her head, and took a deep breath. She glanced at her Papa, who was watching her with a knowing smile. He gave her a sly wink before closing his eyes.

Faith had always been the foundation of the Bernthal family. Her Papa's father, Virginia's Opa John Jakob, had been the pastor at St. Trinity Lutheran Church. Virginia had never met her grandfather in person, as he had passed away six years before her birth, and she felt a connection with him in moments like this. She knew just the blessing to say.

"Abba, Lieber Vater, Amen." ("Papa, loving Father, Amen.")

"Amen," her family responded in unison.

Papa squeezed her hand and leaned in. "Well done, Virginia. Your Opa John would have been so proud of you."

Virginia's face flushed, a pink blush spreading across her cheeks.

She turned to Mama, curiosity burning inside her. "Mama, your table looks so beautiful tonight. The best china, the crystal... and so many of my favorite dishes." She narrowed her eyes, her eyebrows raised. "It feels like a special occasion."

Mama and Papa exchanged a glance, a secret glint in their eyes. Mama turned to Papa. "Nothing escapes these two, does it?"

Papa chuckled. "No, my dear. We've raised children too smart for their own good."

Before Virginia could press further, Robert said, "Not only that, Gin—Oma made her Zimt-

Kaffeekuchen, too!"

Virginia turned to her brother. "I know, Robert. I helped Oma with the baking, didn't I Oma?"

Oma nodded. "That you did meine Zuckermund."

Papa sighed. "You're right, my dear ones. Tonight is a special evening indeed." He paused and turned to his mother-in-law, smiling. "Would you like to do the honors, Tilly?"

Oma dabbed her lips with her crisp linen napkin and set it neatly beside her plate. She then smiled softly at her grandchildren.

"Well," she said. "I suppose there's no point in keeping the secret any longer."

CHAPTER 5

"Meine lieblings, ("My dear ones,") there's no fooling the two of you," Oma said, her eyes twinkling as she glanced between Virginia and Robert. "The Zimt-Kaffeekuchen, the coffee cake Virginia and I baked this afternoon, and the beautiful dinner your Mama prepared indicate it's time for a celebration."

Virginia sat up taller in her chair, proud of herself for solving the mystery. Her curiosity was piqued.

Oma continued gently, "Do you remember when I came here to live with you and your family?"

"Of course," Virginia interjected. "You came when Opa Emil passed. We all miss him very much."

"Yes, ich vermisse ihn auch." ("I miss him too.")

Oma smiled thinking of Opa, but there was a soft sadness in her eyes. "Those were difficult days. But being with family, with you, meine Zuckermund, helped my heart heal. Your Opa fell ill in late summer, which meant I missed two very special birthdays last year."

Virginia looked down at her dinner plate, a lump rising in her throat. "It's alright, Oma. Robert and I understand."

"No, no, meine Liebchen," ("my loves,") Oma insisted, reaching out to clasp Virginia's hand in her own. "Birthdays are important. A birthday *must* be celebrated, and that is precisely what we will do." Her expression brightened. "I felt so lost last October when you turned ten, and when Robert turned eleven. I was so caught up in my grieving that we didn't get to celebrate you properly. So… to correct that error, I have a special adventure planned for Robert tomorrow and one just for Virginia, on Sunday."

Virginia looked up from her plate, her eyes wide.

"Really, Oma?"

Oma smiled. "And knowing how much you love my cinnamon-sugar kuchen," she said, gesturing to the cake on the table, "think of this as your belated birthday cake. But!" She raised a playful finger. "Since you share a birthday, I insist you share this cake as well. Alles Gute zum Geburtstag, meine Lieben." ("Happy birthday, my dear ones.")

Virginia and Robert popped-up from their chairs as if they were spring-loaded, enveloping their Großmutter in a tight embrace.

"Thank you, Oma!" they chorused.

Virginia pressed her face into Oma's shoulder, inhaling her scent: the warm aroma of baking spices, the fresh crispness of soap, and a faint floral hint of violet perfume. It was the scent of home, love, and comfort.

She pulled back slightly, her eyes wide with wonder. "But Oma, what will we do on Sunday?" Already, Virginia's mind was racing with possibilities.

Oma laughed quietly, her eyes glimmering. "Patience, patience, meine Liebling. You will just have to wait and see!"

Virginia glanced at Robert, excitement bubbling between them. As sweet as Oma's coffee cake was, nothing was quite as sweet as the anticipation of a surprise. Virginia could hardly wait.

CHAPTER 6

Time passed like molasses for Virginia the next day.

She woke even earlier than usual, unable to force her eyes shut for even a second longer. The anticipation of Oma's surprise adventure buzzed in her imagination like an alarm clock.

After making her bed, washing her face, and brushing her teeth, she slipped on a crisp white blouse. Next, she pulled on the dark blue cotton overalls that Oma had sewn for her, perfect for weekend play and chores.

Fully dressed, Virginia sat on the edge of her bed and looked down at her well-worn Mary Jane shoes. They had been her shoes for two winters now. After a growth spurt last fall, they were beginning to cramp her feet. Still, she couldn't help but love these shoes with their tan leather and the brown satin ribbon that tied them. *I must admit, friends, you've seen better days,* Virginia thought.

She sighed, then stood up and hurried downstairs to the kitchen, hoping to find Oma in hopes that she might uncover clues about Sunday's adventure.

With enthusiasm, she threw open the kitchen door. "Good morning, Oma! Oma? Oh!"

Instead of Oma, she found Mama sitting at the table, sipping coffee from a fine porcelain teacup adorned with delicate pink flowers and twisting green vines.

Mama smiled. "Good morning my darling. I hope you slept well?"

"Oh yes, Mama, I did."

"You seem surprised to see me. Were you expecting someone else?" Her voice held a teasing lilt.

Virginia hesitated. "Oh, well... I suppose I expected to see Oma this morning. It's so early. Have you seen her?"

Mama took another slow sip of her coffee, drawing out the moment. "Your Oma? Let me think." She set the cup down and pretended to ponder.

Virginia couldn't bear the suspense. "Oh, Mama! Tell me! I know you know where she is! I don't know what I'll do if you don't tell me this very moment!"

Mama laughed gently. "You're right, Virginia. I was just teasing you. Your Oma and Robert had an early morning. I'm afraid you've missed them. They left nearly half an hour ago to catch the first cable car."

Virginia deflated. "But where did they go, Mama? When will they return?"

Mama shook her head. "I'm afraid those secrets are not mine to share, Virginia. You'll just have to be patient."

Frustrated, she huffed. Virginia took pride in knowing *everything* that happened in the Bernthal household. The idea that Oma and Robert were on a mysterious adventure without her was almost too much to bear.

"Mama!" she protested. "What am I to do all day?"

Edna Bernthal knelt before her daughter and lifted her chin so their eyes met. "Today's adventure belongs to your brother, my love. I'm certain he'll tell you all about it when he returns. But for now, you must busy yourself with other things."

Virginia softened. "Like what, Mama?"

"Perhaps you can spend some time on your piano studies. Once you're done, we can select an outfit for your adventure with Oma tomorrow."

Virginia's eyes lit up. "Oh, Mama! Do you know where she's taking me?"

Mama feigned seriousness. "My lips are sealed, Virginia. Your Oma has sworn me to secrecy." She winked and returned to her coffee.

Virginia let out a weary sigh, knowing that further questioning was futile. "Alright, Mama. I'll be in the drawing room, practicing my scales, so you'll know where to find me if you suddenly remember anything you want to share."

With dramatic flair, she turned on her heels. Mama shook her head, smiling to herself. *She has no idea what a wonderful surprise tomorrow holds for her.*

CHAPTER 7

The day continued to drag on, feeling for Virginia as though it might never end.

Mama did her best to help keep her daughter busy. Virginia spent an hour and a half on her keyboard exercises, effortlessly moving from her scales to Bach minuets. The next hour was dedicated to mastering the tricky Rondeau in B-flat Major. As her fingers danced over the keys, Virginia marveled at how time seemed to slip away. The world melted around her when she played, and nothing else mattered but the music.

After practicing, Virginia helped Mama with some household chores. Saturday's primary task was dusting and polishing the woodwork in the front hall—a task Virginia loved, surprisingly. Mama's duster had a long wooden handle and a cluster of soft white turkey feathers. It was just the right length to allow Virginia to reach the picture rail, but only if she stood on her tip-toes. As she dusted, she pretended to be a prima ballerina, gracefully sweeping the duster across the high surfaces as she twirled and spun through the house.

Once she ensured every mahogany surface in the front hall gleamed, Virginia changed the linens on the beds. Then, she kept Mama company while mending clothes at the kitchen table. Papa arrived home shortly after noon, walking in from the office with a tired yet contented smile. The three shared a light lunch: split pea soup and butter sandwiches, made with salted butter spread between slices of Oma's Black Forest Bread—one of Virginia's all-time favorites.

The afternoon continued to creep by slowly. Virginia was nearly finished washing the last luncheon dishes when she heard the front door opening. "Robert! Oma!" she shouted, her heart skipping a beat.

Robert was helping Oma out of her coat when Virginia bolted into the front hall, excitement bubbling up inside her. She quickly wiped her hands on her apron, trying to collect herself. She didn't want to appear over-eager, especially to her older brother. Clearing her throat, she asked, "Did you two have a pleasant day?"

Oma's eyes twinkled with a secret. "We did, Virginia. Robert, would you tell your sister how we spent our day?"

Robert crossed his arms and grinned. "Hmm… I don't know, Oma. Was there anything interesting about today worth mentioning?"

Virginia's patience snapped. With her hands firmly planted on her hips, she marched up to Robert until their noses were nearly touching. "Robert William Bernthal, stop teasing me and tell me what you did today, or I swear…"

Papa's voice broke through, calm but firm. "Virginia…"

She turned to face her father, her eyebrows

furrowed. "But Papa," she grumbled, "I've been so patient all day."

Mama added her voice to the mix. "We'll have plenty of time to hear Bob's story about the day after you finish the delicious supper I spent all day preparing for you. Bob, go wash up. Virginia, I still need your help in the kitchen." She gave them both a pointed look, and the message was clear.

"Yes, Mama," they replied in unison.

Virginia sighed inwardly. She would just have to wait. Again.

When it came time for dinner, Virginia did everything she could to avoid inhaling her food. A few times, she caught Papa's stern yet amused gaze as he watched her eat. His look clearly said, *don't forget to chew, Liebling.*

Once she finished her meal, Virginia placed her knife and fork neatly on her plate, with the fork facing down and the blade inward, just as Mama had taught her. It was a small act of good manners, but one Mama insisted upon. Virginia dabbed the corner of her mouth with her napkin, placed it on her lap, and sat quietly, her hands folded, waiting for everyone else to finish.

Robert was the last to finish his meal, his pace indicating that he was savoring the opportunity to hold his sister hostage. When at long last he placed his silverware across his plate, Papa gave him a pointed look, signaling that it was time to let Virginia off the hook.

Robert's eyes sparkled as he turned to face his sister. "Oh, Gin! You won't believe it. Oma and I had the most marvelous day. We took the streetcar downtown and switched to another line to Lambert Field! We watched the planes taking off and landing, and Oma introduced me to a real-life pilot! It was incredible!"

Virginia's mouth fell open in awe. *Lambert Field!? Airplanes? A real pilot!?* Robert's voice faded into the background as her mind soared into the skies, picturing the planes, the pilot, and the entire adventure.

It wasn't until she realized everyone was staring at her that she returned to reality.

"Gin! Did you hear what I just said?" Robert asked, raising an eyebrow.

Virginia blinked, slightly embarrassed. "Yes, yes, of course, Robert. That does sound like a marvelous day." She turned to face her mother. "Mama, may I be excused?"

Mama smiled sweetly. "Of course, love. Just take your plate to the kitchen, wash up, and don't forget to brush your teeth before bed."

Virginia was out of her chair so fast that it nearly toppled over. "Yes, thank you, Mama. Good night, Papa. Gute Nacht ("Good Night"), Oma. Good night, Robert!" She collected her dinner plate, napkin, and silverware and made a hasty exit to the kitchen, trying her best to contain her excitement.

Papa chuckled as he glanced at Oma. "Are you certain you'll be able to handle that one all day tomorrow?"

Oma's smile was knowing. "Not to worry, William. I am more than equipped to take my granddaughter on our outing tomorrow." She winked at her son-in-law mischievously to punctuate the point.

Upstairs, Virginia had already changed into her pajamas and was pulling her quilt to her chin. "Just one more sleep," she thought, her smile wide. She could hardly wait for tomorrow's adventure.

CHAPTER 8

Early Sunday morning Papa descended the back stairs, hoping to enjoy a quiet cup of coffee before the rest of the family woke up. But at 6:30 a.m., he was startled to find his very animated daughter already in the kitchen.

"Oh! Good morning, Virginia. You're up early."

"Good morning, Papa! Did you sleep well?"

He kissed her on the top of her head. "Yes, Liebling. Thank you—I slept very soundly."

Across the kitchen, Oma was bustling about preparing breakfast. "I've just put on a pot of coffee, William. Es ist fast fertig. ("It's nearly ready.") Virginia and I were discussing the outing we'll take today."

Papa raised an eyebrow. "Oh? Are you having an outing today?" he teased.

"Papa! You know that today is my big day with Oma!" Virginia exclaimed, her eyes brimming with excitement. He smiled warmly at Virginia and tousled her blonde curls. "Yes, of course, Liebling. So, Oma… what is the plan for your big day together?"

Virginia's eyes were locked on her grandmother, hanging on her every word.

"Well," Oma said, smiling, "after breakfast, Virginia will go upstairs and put on the clothes I've laid out for her. Then we'll go… to church."

Virginia's lips parted, preparing to protest. "But Oma…"

Oma interrupted her. "Then *after* church, we will embark on our adventure."

William put his hand reassuringly on his daughter's shoulder. "Virginia, your Oma will share her secrets in due time. For now, I think we should all practice a little patience." He winked at his mother-in-law and gave Virginia's shoulder a gentle squeeze.

"Yes Papa." She sighed, resolved. "Oma, can I help you with breakfast?"

"I thought you'd never ask, meine Zuckermund! I think we should make another of your favorites in honor of this special occasion. Was denken sie?" ("What do you think?")

Virginia's face lit up. "Could we make Zimtschnecken?" Oma's sticky German cinnamon buns were a favorite breakfast treat, second only to Oma's kuchen.

"This is your day, Liebling. If you want Zimtschnecken, then we shall make Zimtschnecken. Fetch your apron. We've got work to do!"

Virginia grinned and turned to Papa, flinging her arms around his waist. "Did you hear that, Papa? You'll have to leave; Oma and I have work to do!"

Papa laughed as he backed out of the room.

"Fine, fine. I don't want to get in the way. But could you please bring me my coffee when it's ready?"

Virginia beamed. "Yes, Papa! Of course! Now, go!"

William only saw Virginia once more before breakfast when she brought him his morning coffee. Otherwise, she was glued to her Oma's side, not wanting to miss a moment.

The family gathered for a modest Sunday breakfast, as they always did before heading across town to St. Trinity Lutheran Church. In the time before Virginia and Robert were born, Papa's father, the Reverend John Jakob Bernthal, had been the pastor there for over thirty years. Virginia loved going to church. She adored the sweeping ivory arches, the smooth polished pews, and the light pouring through the stained-glass windows, casting vibrant colors all around. But most of all, she loved the church's grand pipe organ, which filled an entire wall in a loft at the back of the sanctuary.

The long gold pipes gleamed in the morning

sunlight, and when the organist played the low bass notes, the vibrations rumbled through the entire church, and Virginia felt like she was part of the music itself. Sometimes, she found it hard to focus on the pastor's long sermons, but she couldn't look away whenever the organ was playing. She sat in rapt attention on the edge of her pew, her feet dangling just inches above the floor, lost in the sound.

This Sunday's service ended with one of her Mama's favorite hymns, "A Mighty Fortress is Our God." The guest organist, Mr. Edgar McFadden, traditionally started the piece with four-part harmony. As the second stanza began, Virginia noticed the introduction of a countermelody in the treble line, floating high above the other parts. This light and sweet treble line floated through the sanctuary like butterflies fluttering through the Bernthal's summer garden. *This reminds me of some of Anna Magdalena's melodies,* she thought.

By the third stanza, Mr. McFadden introduced the bass notes of the Kilgen organ. Virginia had been waiting for this moment. She slid forward off the front edge of her pew, her feet finally touching the ground to feel the bass notes' full power. As the organ's deep sounds reverberated through the wooden floorboards of the church, the vibrations danced through her body, making her feel like she was an extension of the music, her entire being resonating with the sound.

Finally, as the fourth and final stanza started, Mr. McFadden pulled out all of the organ's stops, unleashing a powerful blast of unfiltered music. To Virginia, it looked as though he was dancing, his hands flying across the two tiers of keys as he coaxed every note from the organ. *If Heaven has a sound, this is it,* Virginia thought, her heart soaring with the music.

It took all of Virginia's willpower not to burst into applause when the final note rang through the church's rafters. Knowing that polite children did not clap in church, she quickly scooted back onto the pew and sat on her hands to keep them still.

Mama noticed and glanced down at her daughter, a small smile tugging at the corners of her lips. "It appears you enjoyed the music, Virginia."

"Oh yes, Mama, very, very much." She paused, then added, "Do you think I could thank Mr. McFadden for playing so beautifully?"

"Come with me, and I'll introduce you." Oma took Virginia by the arm and led her down the church's center aisle, away from their pew, towards the back wall. As they passed the pulpit, Oma turned left, guiding Virginia to a small white door.

"Up we go!" she said with a wink.

They climbed a narrow flight of stairs, and when they reached the top, Virginia stepped into the choir loft. Looking down over the entire sanctuary, she couldn't help but gasp.

Wow! she thought, her eyes wide with awe. *This is what it must feel like to be an angel.*

CHAPTER 9

R obert waved at his sister from their pew, way down below. Virginia waved back, her face lighting up with a wide smile.

Oma put a hand on Virginia's back and guided them toward the organ, where a handsome man with neat white hair and wire-rimmed glasses was shuffling through a stack of music.

"Edgar!"

The man turned toward Oma's voice. "My goodness! Matilda! I thought I had seen you in the congregation. What a pleasant surprise."

"Oh, Edgar. We've known each other for far too long for you to call me by my full name."

"Of course, Tilly. It's so nice to see you. My condolences on Emil's passing. He was a good man."

Oma nodded solemnly. "Thank you, Edgar. He was quite fond of you." Then, she straightened, turning to her young companion. "Edgar, I would like to introduce you to a very talented young musician. This is my granddaughter, Virginia."

Virginia blushed, suddenly feeling very shy. *Me, a musician?* she thought. She extended her hand with a smile.

"It's very nice to meet you, Mr. McFadden. I enjoyed listening to you play this morning," she said, her voice hesitant but warm.

He shook her hand firmly. "Thank you, Virginia." His hazel eyes twinkled. "It's a pleasure to meet a fellow musician. What instrument do you play?"

Virginia smiled at Oma and turned back to Mr. McFadden. "I don't know that I would call myself a musician just yet, Mr. McFadden, but I do enjoy playing the piano. I've been taking lessons for over four years now."

"Marvelous!" Mr. McFadden exclaimed. "I studied the piano for many years before transitioning to the organ, Virginia. As a pianist, I credit Bach for giving me a solid foundation of the technical skills that have served me well as an organist."

"Bach!" Virginia's eyes widened with excitement. "Mr. McFadden, I'm studying Bach myself. My favorite pieces are from the Anna Magdalena Notebook."

Mr. McFadden stepped back, his head tilting in surprise. "My goodness! Your grandmother's introduction was accurate after all. Despite your modesty, I believe you *are* a serious musician. Keep at it, Virginia. Stay diligent in your studies. Maybe someday we can arrange a time for me to show you the ins-and-outs of this magnificent pipe organ."

Virginia could hardly believe what she was hearing. "Oh, that would be wonderful, Mr. McFadden! Thank you!"

Oma smiled warmly at her old friend. "Thank you, Edgar. It was very kind of you to spend time with us. But I'm afraid Virginia and I must be going. We have an appointment and can't be late."

"Oh!" Mr. McFadden exclaimed. "Please don't let me keep you! May I ask how two distinguished and sophisticated ladies spend their afternoon?"

Virginia looked up at her Oma, her eyes sparkling with anticipation; *this is it!* she thought to herself.

"I'm afraid that's a secret I must keep a little longer, Edgar," Oma said slyly. "But I suspect Virginia will soon want to bend *your* ear about our outing today." She gave her granddaughter a smile before turning back to her old friend. "It's always lovely to see you, Edgar. We must find a time to meet for a longer social call. It's been far too long."

"It was lovely to see you too, Tilly. And yes, I'll find a time to call on you soon." Mr. McFadden smiled at Virginia. "It was a pleasure meeting another musician; I can't wait to hear all about whatever adventure your grandmother has in store for you."

"Thank you, Edgar. Your beautiful music was the perfect prelude to what I'm certain will be a very special day for us. I look forward to seeing you again soon."

Oma nodded to Virginia and turned her toward the door. Virginia glanced over her shoulder.

"Thank you, Mr. McFadden! I hope that someday I can make music as beautiful as yours!"

He smiled, bowed slightly and waved as Virginia and Oma disappeared through the door and made their way down the staircase.

CHAPTER 10

When Virginia returned to their pew, she found her parents waiting for her, but Robert was nowhere to be seen. *He's probably telling his school friends about his airplane adventures,* she thought. Mama and Papa were already holding their coats—Mama held Virginia's coat while Papa held Oma's coat, hat, and purse.

"Come along, Virginia, trödele nicht!" ("don't dawdle!") Mama called, urging her along. "You and Oma have appointments to keep!" Virginia slipped into her winter coat and buttoned it up snugly.

"We expect a great report from your Oma today, Virginia. Be a good girl," Papa said as he gently lifted her chin and kissed her forehead sweetly. "And have *fun.*"

"I will, Papa, I promise," she said. Her parents turned from their pew and walked to the front of the sanctuary, greeting the pastor with warm smiles.

Oma placed her hands firmly on Virginia's shoulders. "Off we go, Liebchen!" she said, a spark of adventure in her smile. She led Virginia back down the aisle and through the front doors of St. Trinity's.

At long last, Virginia thought, *the adventure has begun!*

They walked a few short blocks to the Broadway streetcar line. Oma bought two one-way tickets, and soon they were heading north, with the muddy Mississippi River snaking alongside their path to their east.

"Where are we going, Oma? Please? Can you tell me yet?"

Oma escaped with a soft laugh. "Well, meine Zuckermund, I can't reveal all my secrets, but we are headed downtown for a ladies' matinee luncheon at

Stix, Baer & Fuller. A proper afternoon tea is just the thing we need to fortify ourselves for the adventure ahead."

Virginia's face flushed with excitement. *A matinee luncheon in a fancy downtown department store? How cosmopolitan we are!* she thought to herself.

After several stops, they arrived at their destination, just two blocks from Stix, Baer & Fuller. The grand department store stood at the corner of 6th Street and Washington Avenue, stretching an entire city block and towering eight stories high. Their destination was the newly remodeled tearoom, The Moderne Room.

Oma led Virginia past displays of leather goods, jewelry, and perfume to the heart of the store. She stopped abruptly and turned to Virginia.

"The Moderne Room is on the sixth floor. Now, we face a choice. Would you like to take the passenger elevator, or would you prefer the escalator?"

Virginia hesitated for a moment; both options

seemed thrilling. She had ridden in an elevator when she visited Papa at work, so she chose the escalator. "The escalator, please, Oma."

"To the escalator, lass uns gehen!" ("let's go!")

Virginia and Oma rounded the corner and stood before the polished wooden escalator. Virginia took a deep breath and bravely stepped forward onto a wooden step with Oma following closely behind. As they ascended, they paused at the landing on each floor, waiting for other shoppers with bags full of treasures to make their way up. At long last, they reached the sixth floor.

Virginia stepped off the escalator, finding herself in an elegant lobby decorated in soft shades of jade green and purple orchid. The walls were adorned with fountains and cascading trellises of flowers. *This has to be the most sophisticated place I have ever seen,* she marveled, awestruck.

Oma approached the hostess. "We have a reservation under the name Virginia Bernthal for two at noon. Tea for two!"

"And two for tea!" Virginia giggled to her grandmother. Oma winked, her eyes sparkling.

The hostess led them into a beautifully appointed dining room with soaring Grecian pillars also draped in silk fabric in soft greens and purples. Small tables, each set with white linens and two or four chairs, were scattered around the room. Even though it was early on a Sunday, a good-sized group of ladies had already gathered for tea. The hostess led them to a table in the center of the room, pulling out Virginia's chair first, followed by Oma's.

"A server will be over momentarily with your tea tray," the hostess said before walking away.

Virginia studied the room. "Oma… this is all so beautiful. Thank you for bringing me here. I feel so grown up."

Oma smiled at her granddaughter, her eyes filled with affection. "My sweet Virginia, this is just the *beginning* of our adventure. You could call it the overture. You've been patient since Friday when I announced that we'd spend the day together. I believe it's time to reward that patience."

Virginia's eyes grew wide. She had been so captivated by the opulence of The Moderne Room that she had forgotten this wasn't the surprise Oma had planned.

Oma continued, "I'm very blessed to be Großmutter to two such wonderful children. I feel doubly blessed to live with you and your parents, allowing me to be part of your daily lives. Seeing you and Robert grow into such remarkable young people is wonderful. Es wärmt mein Herz." ("It warms my heart.")

Virginia reached across the table and took Oma's hand. "We love that you live with us, Oma! I wouldn't want it any other way."

"Das bringt mir Freude." ("That brings me happiness.") Oma wiped away a small, happy tear with her napkin before continuing. "And, Liebling, one of the great joys of seeing you and your brother daily is learning about your passions. I've been watching both of you closely these past six months, and your passions have become clear to me. Robert loves science and airplanes, but you, meine Zuckermund—you love music!"

Virginia was surprised by Oma's words and her cheeks flushed. She had never been shy about her love of music, but hearing Oma say it out loud made her feel as if she was glowing on the inside. "Thank you, Oma," she whispered humbly.

"So!" Oma smiled. "What better way for a Großmutter to spoil a grandchild with a passion for music than with a matinee performance by one of the country's great orchestras? When we finish tea, you and I have a date with the Symphony!"

The Symphony! Virginia could barely believe her ears. She had listened to recordings of the London Philharmonic on Mama's phonograph, but to be in the same room with a *real* orchestra was almost more than she could bear. Her excitement made tears well-up in her eyes.

As they enjoyed cucumber sandwiches, scones, teacakes and sips of bitter black Darjeeling tea,

Virginia peppered Oma with a hundred questions about the orchestra. "What music will they play? How long did they practice? Are any of the players women? Do all orchestras play the same music? How do they know when to start and stop?"

Oma answered every question patiently in an attempt to calm her excitable granddaughter. "Deep breaths, Liebling. Deep breaths!"

When the teapot was empty (and Virginia had exhausted her list of inquiries), they put on their coats, took the elevator down six floors, and stepped out the doors of Stix, Baer & Fuller into the crisp February air. Their next destination was the Municipal Auditorium, home to the second-oldest symphonic orchestra in the United States—the St. Louis Symphony Orchestra.

CHAPTER 11

Virginia and Oma arrived at the Municipal Auditorium just in time to find their seats and settle in for the afternoon concert.

Stix, Baer & Fuller may have impressed Virginia, but it didn't hold a candle to the majestic beauty of St. Louis' Municipal Auditorium. The building's exterior was a masterpiece, blending Art Deco with Classic Revival Style. It was clad entirely in limestone, and towering above them were eight grand, multi-story Corinthian columns. Two enormous Missouri limestone bears stood on pedestals by the front entrance, two stone sentinels standing guard. To Virginia, Municipal Auditorium looked like a palace—*precisely* what she imagined a home for an orchestra should look like.

Once inside, they passed through the Grand Foyer. Their footsteps echoed on the polished marble floors, which sparkled with golden inlays underfoot. Virginia's eyes widened. "Wow, it's even grander inside," she whispered.

The air was filled with the excitement of people arriving. The matinee crowd was dressed in elegant coats and dresses, and were chatting in hushed voices. Virginia could hardly believe she was here. Every step she took seemed to lead her deeper into a dream world.

They climbed a small set of stairs and were greeted at the top by a friendly usherette. Virginia, standing behind Oma, couldn't help but study her. The usherette, perhaps only a few years older than Virginia, wore a sharp black wool uniform with a high-collared jacket, brocade piping, and a skirt flared just below her knees. She wore black tights and shiny black Mary Jane shoes, identical to the shoes Virginia was wearing.

What a lucky girl, Virginia thought, *to be surrounded by all this beautiful music. Someday…*

The usherette collected their tickets, carefully tore

them, and handed two stubs back to Oma. She smiled and passed one to Virginia. "Here, my dear, keep this as a memento of our special day." Virginia tucked the stub into her coat pocket, her heart swelling with excitement.

Virginia's jaw dropped as they followed the usherette into the Opera House.

The room stretched before them—an ocean of deep green velvet seats.

"Oma! The Opera House is enormous! Are there really that many people in all of St. Louis?" Virginia gasped; her voice filled with wonder.

Oma chuckled and turned to her. "Would you believe me if I told you there are over three thousand seats here, meine Zuckermund?" She winked, guiding her granddaughter further into the hall. "And soon, every seat will be filled with music lovers."

Virginia's eyes grew even wider. The thought of three thousand people all sharing the same musical experience sent a thrill through her.

The usherette led them closer to the stage, stopping

in Row H. "Here you are," she said, pointing to their seats. "The concert will begin shortly!" With a final wave, she returned to her post.

As they navigated the aisle toward their seats, Virginia became so distracted by the grandeur around her that she accidentally stepped on a few toes. *Oops,* she thought. Hearing a chorus of polite repetitions of "excuse me" and "sorry." Oma turned to Virginia and said gently, "Just focus on where you're walking, Virginia. You will have plenty of time to take in this place's beauty once you are settled in your seat."

Virginia nodded and took a deep breath, finally returning to their seats. They removed their coats and sat down. Virginia sank into the plush velvet of her seat, feeling as if she entered a world that was nothing like her everyday life.

Before her, the Opera House stage was set. Red velvet curtains framed the stage, and the music stands lined up in neat, concentric arcs. She tried to count the chairs—fifty? No… sixty? Seventy? A hundred? She lost count. *How many musicians are in this orchestra?* she thought.

As she was mentally tallying, musicians began to enter the stage from a small door on the right, each dressed in a sharp black tuxedo and carrying an instrument. Virginia couldn't help but notice that every single musician was a man. *Hmm…I wonder why that is?* she thought.

Her curiosity pulled her back into the present. "Oma, what's that long instrument that looks like a wooden tube?" Virginia asked, pointing toward the unfamiliar instrument.

Oma leaned in to get a better look. "Ah, that would be a bassoon, Liebling," she explained.

Bassoon…bassooooon. Virginia liked the sound of that. *It has a mysterious quality to it.*

"Oma," Virginia asked, "do you know what piece the orchestra will be playing this afternoon?"

"It's a new concerto by George Gershwin," Oma replied.

"Gershwin? I think I heard that name before…"

"I do believe you have," Oma said with a smile.

"You know that record from your Mama's collection?"

She usually listened to Bach's music more than anything else, but she was certain that the name George Gershwin was one she'd seen before.

"Yes! The record with *'I've Got Rhythm'* and *'Rhapsody in Blue'* on it, correct?"

Before Oma could respond, the lights dimmed. A spotlight lit the stage door, and the conductor, a tall, elegant man in a tuxedo with tails entered. The audience clapped politely as he walked to the center stage, bowed gracefully, and then turned to face the orchestra.

The conductor took his place at the podium, his baton ready. The violinist on his left raised his bow and played a single, long note. Gradually, the string players joined in, tuning their instruments individually, followed by brass and woodwinds. When the tuning concluded, the room fell silent. The air buzzed with the collective anticipation of the audience. Virginia held her breath.

CHAPTER 12

The conductor scanned the faces of the players in front of him, raised a slender baton, and as it hovered in the air it was as if time in the Opera House had suddenly stopped.

In the stillness, Virginia noticed the rapt attention of the musicians on the stage. Each of them sat upright, rigid in their chairs, instruments poised in their hands, their eyes locked on the conductor's baton with laser focus attention. She couldn't explain it, but she had never heard silence so *loud* before; it was absolutely deafening. She sat in breathless anticipation, and then, with a sudden, dramatic downward sweep of the baton, the music of Gershwin's *Piano Concerto in F Major* came to life and flooded Virginia's senses.

As the first notes of the concerto filled the hall, Virginia's heart soared; she had *never* heard music like this before and it delighted her. The opening measures were undeniably classical in nature, yet there was something sparkly, no *bubbly* about them; an energy that made the rhythms pulse through her body with life and vitality. She closed her eyes and took a deep breath in.

Within seconds Virginia was transported into a world of sound and rhythm as the music flowed around her. The gleaming tympani (which looked like oversized versions of the kettles in Mama's kitchen) rumbled, sending vibrations through her entire body, the same feeling she had experienced listening to the pipe organ at church earlier that morning. *Boom-boom-boom-boom, boom-boom-boom-boom.*

She heard the familiar, shimmering voices of the violins, but their melodies were intertwined with the cries of trumpets, trombones and something else. She couldn't identify the instrument she was hearing. *What was it?* she thought. *Is that a clarinet?* The mystery instrument cried out for her attention, the melody bright and clear in the air. She searched her memory, remembering the same sound when she'd first heard Gershwin's music on Mama's record. *Yes, that's a clarinet,* she affirmed. *I remember the same sound in the opening measures of Rhapsody in Blue.* She was proud of herself for having solved the mystery, and sat a little taller in her seat.

She was pulled back to her senses by a sudden virtuosic melody taken over by the piano—not just any piano, but a long, sleek concert grand, more elegant than any piano she'd ever seen. The grand piano's black lacquered case glistened under the stage lights, and the lid was held aloft with a narrow stick that allowed Virginia to see the golden strings inside. The piano melody was so percussive and rhythmic Virginia couldn't help but keep time by tapping her fingers on her knees.

When the first movement ended, Virginia nearly flew out of her seat. The steady building of overlapping rhythms, melodies and harmonies tugged at her. Sensing her granddaughter's elation, Oma gently reached over and put a hand on Virginia's hands, both to calm her, but also to prevent her from applauding prematurely. "Stetig," ("Steady,") she whispered. "We have two movements yet to go before we can clap." Virginia nodded and settled back into her seat.

The second movement was slower and more introspective, making Virginia feel as though she were floating. The melodies intertwined like an intimate dance, with each instrument gracefully passing the lead to the next. She closed her eyes tight as she listened, trying to visualize the notes in her mind; each note seemed to perfectly unfold, falling into place in an elegant musical equation. She couldn't help but notice comparisons to the pieces in her beloved *Anna Magdalena Notebook*.

Then came the final movement, the *Allegro Agitato*. The jazzy rhythms built to a fever pitch, filling the air with an indescribable energy. Virginia's heart pounded in sync with the music, her body trembling with excitement as the orchestra reached a wild, dramatic crescendo. The piece ended with a glorious cacophony of sound, prompting the entire audience to spontaneously leap to their feet. This time, Oma didn't impede her granddaughter's impulse, and Virginia rose to her feet clapping wildly for the musicians on the stage.

Oma stood too, and as she glanced down at her granddaughter, she was surprised to see tears rolling down Virginia's cheeks. She turned and sweetly cupped her companion's face in her hands, wiping a tear from her cheek with a graceful sweep. "Meine Liebchen, what's wrong? Why are you crying?"

Virginia beamed through her tears. "I'm just so… so happy," she whispered, the music still ringing in her ears. She threw her arms around her grandmother, squeezing her tightly. "Danke, Oma. Danke schön," ("Thank you, Oma. Thank you very much,") she whispered.

As the applause echoed in her ears, Virginia knew this was only the beginning of her musical adventures.

They held each other tightly as the roar of the crowd continued around them. In that moment, the love between grandmother and granddaughter—a bond that transcended generations—felt even more powerful.

It's just as Hans Christian Andersen said, Oma thought to herself as she held Virginia close, *where words fail, music speaks.*

Oma's German Glossary

I n this story, you will have noticed dialogue in two different languages: English and German. Virginia's family was of German descent, so even though her family lived in America, German was still a language that was spoken in the Bernthal household, particularly by the older generations.

Today, an estimated 155 million people speak German, making it the 11th most spoken language in the world.

Historically, 1936 was a very tense time in global politics. World War I had ended in 1918, and the Second World War would begin in 1939, just three years after this story is set. Germany's part in World War I led to widespread anti-German sentiment in the United States. Propaganda in the press portrayed German Americans as uncivilized, materialistic, and aggressive. Many Americans were concerned that German Americans were a threat to American values.

For these reasons, Virginia's family would have only spoken the German language in places where there were other German-speaking people, and where it felt safe: at home or in church. In this story, Oma uses German phrases to show affection for her family, particularly her grandchildren.

Below is a Glossary of the German words and phrases that are used in *Virginia B. Goes to the Symphony.*

German Words and Phrases	English Translations
Großmutter/Grossmutter	Grandmother
Oma	The more casual equivalent of Grandma
"Ich bin in der küche. Begleite mich."	"Join me in the kitchen."
Meine Zuckermund	My little sugar mouth or my little sweet tooth
Großfater/Grossfater	Grandfather

Opa	The more casual equivalent of Grandpa
"Mein Gott in Himmel! Wie Kann das sein?"	An expression of surprise: "My God in Heaven! How can this be?"
"Wenn du darauf bestehst."	"If you insist."
Zimt kaffeekuchen	cinnamon coffee cake
"Du machst mich stolz."	"You make me proud."
"Lassen sie mich sehen."	"All right, let me see."
"Ich erinnere mich!"	"I remember!"
"Du bist schalu!"	"You're clever!"
"Bist du zicher?"	"Are you certain?"
"Ya, ich bin mir sicher."	"Yes, I am certain."
"Braves Mädchen."	"Good girl."
"So klug."	"So smart."
"Geduld, miene liebe."	"Patience, my love."
Sauerbraten	A marinated beef roast served with a sweet-sour gravy.
Abba, Lieber Vater, Amen.	A prayer: Papa, loving father, thank you.

Meine leiblings	My dear ones
"ich vermisse ich auch."	"I miss him, too."
Miene liebchens	A term of endearment: my loves
fiere dich	celebrate you
"Alles Gute zum Geburtstag, mein Liebers."	"Happy Birthday, my dear ones."
Trödele nicht!	don't dawdle/ hurry up!
"lass uns gehen."	"let's go."
"Es wärmt mein herz."	"It warms my heart."
"Das das macht mich froh."	"That brings me happiness."
Und dein bruder	and your brother
meine kleine	A term of endearment: my little one
stetig	Be steady
"Danke, Oma. Danke schön."	"Thank you, Oma. Thank you very much."

Virginia's Journal Reflection Pages

1. What is your favorite part of Virginia's story, and what makes it special to you?

_____

_____

_____

_____

_____

2. What are some ways Virginia's family members show love and support for one another? Does anyone in your life remind you of them?

_____

_____

_____

_____

_____

3. Did anything in this story remind you of a tradition or special moment from your own family or culture?

_____

_____

_____

_____

_____

4. If you could ask Virginia one question about her adventure, what would it be and why?

_____

_____

_____

_____

_____

5. Did you learn any moral or values from this book? If yes, what were they?

_____

_____

_____

_____

_____

6. How do Virginia's actions reflect good character, even when things don't go her way? Have you ever shown good character?

_____

_____

_____

_____

_____

7. How does music affect Virginia in this story? Why do you think music is so meaningful to her?

_____

_____

_____

_____

_____

8. Have you ever heard live music, like a symphony or concert? How did it make you feel? If not, what would you imagine it feels like?

_____

_____

_____

_____

_____

Optional Drawing or Creative Space:

Use this space to sketch a picture, write a short poem, or create your own story inspired by *Virginia B. Goes to the Symphony.*

Keep this journal close! As Virginia continues
her adventure, so can you!

Are you ready for Virginia B.'s next big adventure?

Get ready to take flight with the second book in the Virginia B. series!

It's 1937, and all of St. Louis is buzzing about the event of the season—the St. Louis Air Races! At Horace Mann Elementary, students are going plane-crazy… and Virginia B. is no exception. But there's just one problem: girls aren't exactly encouraged to love science.

So… what's a curious, big thinker like Virginia to do?

In *Virginia B. and the Wings of Wonder*, imagination soars as she discovers a new passion for science and flight—and makes some surprising new friends along the way.

Virginia B. and the Wings of Wonder

Coming Soon!

Author Kevin Pease

Kevin first discovered the magic of storytelling when he was cast as the pickle in his elementary school play, *The Sandwich*. Since then, he's devoted his life to finding and telling stories—both his own and other people's. As an adult, he has traveled the world collecting tantalizing tales, amazing anecdotes, and fantastic fables. When he's not chasing the next great narrative, Kevin works in education and the arts, inspiring others to use their storytelling superpowers to change the world for the better. He lives in the Windy City with his favorite human, Zachary, and their cat, Charlie. (He also really loves pickles.)

Illustrator Gabriel Gigliotti

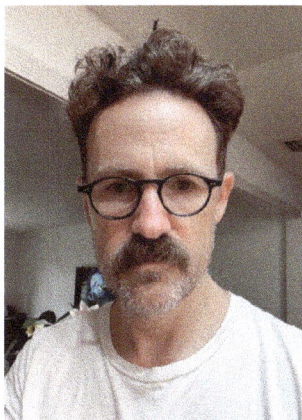

Gabriel Gigliotti attended Parsons School of Design, where he studied fine art. He taught figure drawing at an art school for several years and has illustrated a couple of graphic novels, dozens of magazine and web articles, and a wide range of projects—from children's portraits and film storyboards to mechanical hips for medical catalogues. Gabriel paints every day and lives with his wife and three children in Los Angeles.

Virginia B.

For the latest Virginia **B.** news, including book release dates, special events, and exclusive behind-the-scenes updates, join the Virginia **B.** Clubhouse by visiting:

www.readvirginiab.com

Follow us on social media: Instagram, Facebook, and YouTube: **@readvirginiab**